Bare Spirit

Also by Susan Marshall

Fiction

The Adira Cazon Literary Mystery Series:
Adira and the Dark Horse

Poetry

Evergold Dream

Trekking an Age of Light

Yesterday's Wisdom

Plays

The Theatre Playscapes series:

Fleur of Yesterday

All the Hope We Carry

Single, Full-length Plays:

Indigo's Haven

Broken World

Essays & Articles

Theatre Playscapes: A New Theatrical Style

Theatre Playscapes of Hope

Bare Spirit

The Selected Poems of
Susan Marshall

For the Spirit: may it always be alight with life.

Published in Australia in 2024 by
Story Playscapes
Victoria, Australia
ABN 62197863313

publications@storyplayscapes.com
www.storyplayscapes.com

Copyright © Susan Marshall, 2024

All rights reserved. Apart from any fair dealing for the purposes of private study, research, criticism or review as permitted under the Copyright Act, no part of this publication may be translated, adapted, performed, reproduced, stored in a retrieval system or transmitted in any forms by any means, electronic, mechanical, photocopying, recording or otherwise, without the written permission of the publisher.

This book is a work of fiction. The names, characters, places and events are products of the author's imagination and any resemblance to actual persons or events, past or present, is entirely coincidental.

 A catalogue record for this book is available from the National Library of Australia

Title: Bare Spirit: The Selected Poems of Susan Marshall
Author: Susan Marshall
ISBN: 9780645404166
Subjects: Poetry / Australian & Oceanian
           Body, Mind and Spirit / Inspiration & Personal Growth
           Body, Mind and Spirit / Mindfulness & Meditation

Produced by Story Playscapes
Written by Susan Marshall
Compiled by Susan Marshall
Book design, illustration and photography by Ryan Marshall

All images and text are Copyright © Story Playscapes

The opinions expressed in this publication are those of the author and do not necessarily reflect those of the views of Story Playscapes. While all reasonable checks have been made to ensure the accuracy of statements and advice, no responsibility can be accepted for errors, omissions or representations, express or implied. The author and Story Playscapes do not, under any circumstance, accept any responsibility or loss occasioned to any person acting or refraining from action as a result of material in this publication.

Warning: This book contains mature content, including: adult themes, violence and sexual references. It is not intended to be read by any persons under 18 years of age.

Contents

8	Bare Spirit
10	Shedding at Shore
12	Raw Flute
16	Seeking Sanctuary
18	Spirit Tree
22	Bare Nocturne
24	Lost in Your Wonder
28	Sky Bound
30	Heart's Walk
32	Pebbled Grief
34	Awakening North
38	Road Block
42	Seeing Life Through the Bleak
44	Mind Time
46	Whispering Wind
48	Ever Changing Rhythms of Life
50	Spring's Touch
52	A Writer's Company
54	My Beautiful Mother
56	Pearl Melody
58	Letter Jumble
60	Trekking an Age of Light
62	Dusk Heart
64	Bare Desire
68	Kite Day
70	New Clay Linen
74	Atlas' Groove
78	Warrior Spirit
84	Flying Free
88	Evergold Dream
124	About the Author
127	Acknowledgements
127	About the Book Designer
128	About Story Playscapes

Bare Spirit

If light is a dance,
let its ribbons unfurl
and unravel in
the pervading darkness.

Let my heart's warmth
glow an amber-rose,
soothing
and soaring
my spirit.

I can transcend my place,
soaring up into the aether.
Weightless and free twirling,
surrounded by glowing ribbons,
elated with timeless freedom.

Let my body lines stretch
and exhale their burdens,
releasing negative energy
and absorbing tranquil joy.
Lighter
and lighter,
lines can blur
into the radiant atmosphere,
allowing my spirit to wander.

Let my bare spirit
unravel
like ribbons of
neon light,
unfurling its presence
in the vibrant aether.

As its energy soars,
my bare spirit
can streamline
its journey.
Neon lights pulsing
and flashing
across the dark.

May the dark
shrink to a tiny,
microscopic dot,
overcome by
my bright
neon joy.

Shedding at Shore

Bare foot and outstretched,
facing the heat seared wind.
A sun kissed torso adorned
with pure, white lit sand.

Sands of smouldering time
in love's burning desire.
Two bodies once entwined
upon scorching shore line.

Waves crest as angrily,
as arms that pushed away.
A boat now adrift at sea,
distancing itself greatly.

My airy silk dress blown,
unravelling its gusty anguish.
Fighting against wind's blasts,
clinging tightly to my skin.

Wind ripped silk swept
through the raw air.
Patches of my skin naked,
scorched by harsh light.

Bare spirit facing shore,
frothy and icy white.
Soul sinking in sand's sighs,
light subdued by sea water.

Alone with the aftermath
of anger's lingering flame.
A smouldering stark silence
that festers deep within.

Eyes staring upwards,
meeting sun's glare.
Shutting lids to attune
to red's rhythmic rage.

Lips parched with thirst
after day's lone treks.
Weakened body broken,
solo in its burdens.

A beaten body dropping,
digging nails into sand.
Cooler holes that pulse
with promises of refuge.

Defeated, yet determined
to escape lingering lairs.
The rageful red shouting sky,
the sensually sandy shore.

Waving a silk dress flag
across wind's symphony.
Sending feathers flocking
in an arc across the wind.

Chasing the birds' trails,
across icy, white sea water.
Bouncing anguish's aches,
across ocean's soothing waves.

Bare spirit, now journeying
across the sandy shoreline.
A soul soaring very high
above the sorrowful sand.

Raw Flute

The wind is wild,
the elm tree bare.
Its naked branches
reaching for light.

On bended knee I crouch,
rocking my body
as I stare at the
red scarred moon.

The flute note is raw,
piercing through the wind.
Its sad pitch reverberates
through my bones.

I feel you now,
your spirit is present.
Your raw flute aches
deep within my soul.

Our moments linger,
tearing at my heart.
Our bare bodies once wrapped
in a smouldering embrace.

Search lights protruded
our warm love fire.
Stomping horse hooves
windswept you away.

My scream was shrill,
cutting through night's air.
My arms reaching for
the you I couldn't have.

A single candle remains,
a symbol of our love.
Against wind's wrath it burns
with the strength of a warrior.

My fingers sting
as I burn our letters.
I watch them disintegrate
into black, floating ash.

The candle flame flickers
its yellow eyes to envision,
my journey to safe refuge
away from wind's wrath.

Standing, I stare
out at blood's canvas.
A home torn apart
by wild wind's rage.

The flute note is raw,
I feel your warm embrace.
It helps to dissipate
my deep buried ache.

The elm tree sways
its stark, naked branches.
Our raw love memory remains
and the flute note aches.

Into the black I step,
my feet shaking nervously.
Our burning candle
lights my pathway.

Steadfast and true,
our spiritual bond lives.
We travel together
across wind's wrath.

If night is black ink,
let it write our new fortune.
May our spirits find refuge
in wind's calmer breeze.

Seeking Sanctuary

Sweet new buds, welcome to life.
I see you glisten with morning's dew.
May your brightness help me see
more colour on this very dark road.
I have walked these steps each day,
dodging the serious, watchful gazes
who check if a friend or enemy plays
in this new world of hide and seek.

My pockets are full of thought trails
that crawl into the asphalt cracks.
Street, you whisper loudly today,
waiting for me to find you again.
You have been lost to my heart,
which I did shut away last week.
Burying myself under the ground,
I stared silently at the pitch black.

The hole I dug was safe and small,
protecting me from the other side.
I huddled, eyes wide and awake,
ears alert to any sudden sound.

The air raids would startle me,
intruding upon my silent state.
Hiding in corners of the black,
I dodged the curfew torch lights
and the shuffle of loud footsteps.

I ate the very last food scraps,
starving for the light up above.
That was when I saw you new buds,
your stems reaching into the dark.

You let me climb you to the light,
revealing a vibrantly lit space.
Escaping from the dark shadows,
I discovered refuge in a sanctuary.
Its garden displayed a myriad of
colourful bursts of flowers in bloom.
Nestling into the bed of lavender,
I closed my eyes for the first time ...
since the world changed.

I consider where you might play now,
as I lay staring out at the horizon.
Plucking a petal, I whisper a message
and let it float into the gentle breeze.
The words will drift out of the garden,
across the changed roads we used to tread.
Circling new ground to find their feet,
they will learn a new language to speak.

May my footsteps lighten as I walk
through this new garden sanctuary.
If new spring flowers do rise and bloom,
please let them share our messages ...
of hopes and dreams.

Spirit Tree

A glaring fog leers,
smothering stark air
with the stench of smoke.
It ascends sharply,
masking the intense gaze
of the woman who stares.

Midnight eyes, she has,
blending with the dark.
Camouflaging her spirit
amongst jet ink night.

The asphalt is cracked
and very crisply cold,
abandoned by many feet
who once kept it warm.
Shaking silently she hides
her fear deeply inside
as she awaits the time.

Traces of light glow
in windows unmasked
as night descends upon life.
One such window was hers,
a number of days ago,
before she was hunted down.

In hiding she resides,
her spirit buried within,
wound tightly like a ball.
It rolls aimlessly across asphalt,
street sweeping the debris,
in search of clues.

Thick fog sweeps passed her,
dramatically dissipating away.
She exhales a relieved breath
and stretches her branched arms,
allowing finger leaves to shoot free.

Her trunk stands slowly,
worn out and very wise,
sighing as it sways unsteadily.
Feet flex and unwind,
rooting her firmly into
her home ground's earth.

Her steadfast trunk
battles the frightful fog,
hiding in plain sight,
keeping watch over her family.

Her spirit tree sways,
as the night darkens deeper
and her eyes brighten with
moonlight's magnificent glow.

She stretches her arm branches
towards her daughter's window,
meeting her glowing gaze above.

*Shed your own leaves, child,
let them drop to the ground
until you land in a pile
at my very worn roots.*

*I will gather you in my branches
and carry your far away from here.
We will earth our new roots
somewhere safe and new.*

Bare Nocturne

Bare nocturne's sea sways,
scattering salty spray.
The hour blinks its eyes
like your intense green gaze,
as I step across the tide.

Moon's shadow gleams
a halo around its waning.
A signal for me to retreat
into the rhythmic waters.
A time to release my desires,
across the cresting waves.

Bare nocturne gleams,
a canopy of star light above.
A pent up constellation
of our restrained love.
Buried spirits we've become,
forbidden by our families
to surrender to our desires.

Immersing myself in sea,
my naked body begins to cool.
Water laps across my torso,
like your gentle fingers
as they caress my bare skin.

Moaning, I arch back,
my body tingling wildly.
The wind whispers
its soothing warmth,
like your gentle kisses
across my bare breasts.

Aroused, I meet your gaze,
burning and alluring,
melting my defenses.
Your mouth is warm,
soft lips to kiss deeply.

Our bare torsos connect
within sea's soothing waves.
Bare nocturne burns brightly,
stars burning with deep desires,
like those that stir in my loins.

Lying back in wavy water,
I feel it pool around my loins.
Moaning, I arch back,
willing you to enter me.

Surrendering my desire to you
as the sparkling stars explode.
Crying out, in waves of ecstasy,
as your passion floods me,
like the giant, soaring waves.

Embracing you tightly,
soothed by your heartbeat.
United we are, in love,
away from rivalry's rage.

We continue to float together,
saturated by welcoming waves.
Absorbing nocturne's radiance,
adrift and content at sea.

Lost in Your Wonder

Light dappling in the windows.
Soft, caressing dawn light,
raising life upon your skin.

Reaching for you,
aching.
Heart to heart,
bodies burning,
hot heat
of love.

Mellow, yet content,
your dimple flashes,
lips smiling warmly.

Fragrant pink rose,
you tuck in my hair,
aroma sweet
and lingering ...
with hope.

I am lost in your wonder,
your pool
of mystery
swirling in your eyes.

Your hand in mine,
an age of bliss
and miles
of wander across
lands we dare.

A hill top at sunrise,
your hand on my cheek,
pulling me close ...
your warm, soft lips,
my fevered love.

Rain drops heavily
thud thud
like rage
in you
as you stand.

Earth spins,
sitting me up,
staring
at you ...
leaving.

The absence of you,
ground stark,
silent,
stagnant of life.

My mind frozen,
body cold,
shaking
with sadness.

My heart empty,
missing your life,
your warmth,
your touch.

Your hand I reach for,
its memory,
petals crumbling,
cascading
onto grass.

Reaching across
the abyss,
thrashing through
currents of pain.

Storm pelts,
rain drums heavily.
Floods my eyes
with tears.

Sinking deeply
into stalks
of sadness.

Lost in your ...
wonder.

Sky Bound

The air is fresh,
cool on the skin.
A hint of sun peeks
out from white clouds.
I stand in its glow,
warming myself, drifting ...
sky bound.

Upwards
the birds fly
in a flock in the blue.
Clouds shift at a steady
momentum, catching ...
a single breath.

I inhale cool air,
it racks my chest,
forcing me to cough.
Looking down,
my eyes are glistening.

My feet stand in grass
mowed and wet,
drops of water shine.
It has rained,
so have my eyes.

The sky pictures remain,
my mind shifts
image to image
like travel memories
to exotic countries,
awaiting my steps to
discover ...

A new way
after
the rain ...
with you.

Heart's Walk

The roaring, flickering ashes of fire
did engulf the soft spark of gold
light that once shone in my eyes.
My vision now burns blue and complex,
as I trample the leaves of Autumn,
which fall heavily in this morning haze.
Leaves I used to pick up and toss
high into the free air above me.
A freedom I once lived a life ago,
running across the grassy plain
towards the carefree unknown.

I have met with new lands unclad and free,
along with the birds that flutter a breeze
across my heavy shoulder's weight.
The chirping would carry me along
allowing a chance to forget my burdens
as I walked into a promising new sunrise.

What world would I be met with today?
I would ask myself as I roamed
my land with tender, shaking feet.
Surfaces I trod upon were torn,
ripped apart with my giant footsteps
of so very many questions.

For what is a life that isn't shared,
no matter its fortune or hardships?
Whatever worn bric-a-brac remains
is a trail to follow into a human heart.

As I age, I walk in search of my heart,
which I did once leave lying on top
of a fluttering, black flag cloth.
It rested upon the rooftop of the house
that I spent a long while shuffling in.
A home filled with the clutter of life lived
and captured in its own bric-a-brac.
A life built and lived as one could be,
playing in the new world so freely.

A life once shared and now lived alone,
still reaching out towards the unknown.

Pebbled Grief

Walking dawn my steps are heavy,
the pebbles skirting into my heart.
Stones that are my weight of grief,
remnant dust of life once lived.

The street is a whir with silhouettes,
spinning through the sands of time.
They step upon this ground so freely,
unafraid of treading the path past.

A ragged breath I take with me,
jumping over cracks of memory.
I cannot bare my soul to face,
deep pain searing past steps.

Traces of her still breathe here,
within the dust of life as lived.
Cement does crunch and crack,
leaving crevices buried deep.

Alone, our walls held us true,
our story unfolding silently.
Away, the world a blur be,
unreachable to our lost hearts.

We aged quickly among tunes
of life distant and dancing on.
Our own waltz stumbled afraid
of what world was left to face.

Her last words still echo deeply,
across the too long path I tread.
Begin anew, ignore the ache,
find a way to fill the cracks.

Her words spluttered tissue red,
as her own steps began to fade.
Reaching for her hand once more,
I held it until the finale of day.

The new day is bleak and scarred,
without her I cannot tread further.
These fractured cracks do linger,
sinking my heart with pebbled grief.

If I could learn to walk again,
to meet the gaze of silhouette.
I may find another kindred soul,
to tell me when the blur ends.

Awakening North

Light patches shift across the streets,
awakening my memories of the north.
The very place in which I was born
and as a young man did return to.

I once stood upon the north's dappled streets
and watched the shades of everyday pass.
I was swept across the loose cobble stones,
passed the heavy doors that were bolted shut.

A stranger I was to the folk of the north,
sweeping through their manicured streets.
Stepping across their private grounds,
asking too many important questions.

One day a street began to unravel,
opening a door that had been bolted.
Out stepped you, wise, beautiful lady,
speaking to me in a hoarse whisper.

Your manicured lawn did dissipate,
revealing a garden dug with holes.
Secrets germinated deep within,
blossoming into botanical madness.

A mix of grass stalks and fallen leaves,
swept single letters across the ground.
Digging and planting them into the dirt,
you helped me bring earth to my words.

Words that had eaten away at my core,
like an earthworm at a rotten apple.
Spelling out my deep and mixed feelings
about our very difficult situation.

The sound of circus music began to strum
within the depths of my broken heart.
A sound awakening my childhood being
in the north with you a long time ago.

For there you stood holding my hand,
while we watched the clowns on stilts.
Peering at them from below the stalls,
waiting for them to finally dismount.

Catching a quick view of the clowns
as they dashed back to change costumes.
Looking for the one man we needed
to help us keep up food and house.

He chose to jump into a painted caravan
and whirl away to another circus land.
Walking the world upon tall stilts,
leaving us to stare in tense silence.

And so my childhood did wean away
as I became a young man very quickly.
While I worked hard on the railway tracks,
I considered a life beyond the north.

One day you handed me a wrapped bundle,
kissed me on the cheek and wished me well.
You sent me off to venture out way beyond
the north I had shared with you for so long.

In the bundle were small single words
that shared a very special message.
Words that my voice had never spoken
but that you, my mother, felt I deserved.

Love life right now and not later,
as the days will keep marching on.
Return here when the time is right
and we will share stories once more.

This message I always carry with me
as I venture out from my home north.
Keeping your words close to my heart,
giving me the confidence to explore.

Road Block

The road is long tonight,
darkness digs into potholes,
seeking refuge from stark light.
Asphalt that holds my secrets,
stories I have shared privately
as I continue to face this road.

The dashed road lines glare
like harsh torch light,
forcing direction upon me.
I have followed the lines before,
unaware of their destination,
now caught in these crossroads.

Gravel and road dust mark
my very taught torso.
Marks that have worn away
at my stressed skin over time.
The road tattoos are symbols
of stages of my life faced solo.

Road Block

The rising, raw air is refreshing,
keeping me awake as I watch
the green light flashing ahead.
A symbol to go, to move on,
to continue on a journey that suits.

I have not found solace yet.
My spirit is restless, unsettled,
still peering into that pothole,
hoping to find a solution.
My deep dark tales reside in there,
each one a new deliberation,
an uncertainty or a core fear.

My stifled energy engulfs me,
fogging my very tired brain,
blinding my vision to the light
I need to source in order to heal.

I am connected to this road,
this reliable, permanent fixture.
It is a place that stores my fears
safely away for a time
when I am brave enough
to release them.

Decisions are difficult when solo.
My inner spirit has curled up
into a very tense, tight ball,
unwilling to release its burdens.

I must shed myself of the gravel and dust,
allow it to wash away in this falling rain.
I raise my arms as it pours down open me,
a welcome relief in this strangled air.

My skin is smeared with muddy remnants
of my solo and secret treks of growth.
A world I need to depart, yet will revisit
at another stage in my life.

Cleansed, I feel my spirit is lighter
and beginning to unravel again.
Silently, I will it to release its burdens
and to rise higher, above this road.

Taking one last glance at the pothole,
I farewell my secrets, satisfied to depart.
I have shed this stage of the road,
ready to take some new steps
along a new pathway ...
and see where it leads me.

Seeing Life Through the Bleak

On the back of a fairy wren bird,
sits an ornate, golden pear fruit.
Upon it rests a tiny musical lute
that strums a medieval tune.

The pear evokes visions of chalices,
in which cider happily swishes.
It helps the people chat and drink,
revealing their hardships in a tavern.

Brown and blue wings spanned wide,
the fairy wren flutters its feathers,
cocking its head and gazing out
towards a blooming medieval garden.

The musical lute plays at high pitch,
evoking visions of running across grass,
gathering and harvesting grown herbs
to use for a very soothing banquet.

The pear could feed a crowd of jesters,
who have arrived to play for the Queen.
Its salad could add zing to their tales,
allowing them to chuckle and swing.

Harp strings plucked with exuberance,
jesters would share the people's desires,
to live a life free of such dark illness
in one's life beyond medieval times.

A flock of fairy wrens could land
on grass stalks in the medieval garden.
Splendidly whistling their fine stories,
fluttering their wings before the Queen.

The golden pear could be their gift,
a very rare find in a world so bleak.
The pear could be placed into the lap
of the very tired and aged Queen.

The pear's small voice could be wise,
sharing the wisdom it had gleaned,
sitting on the back of a fairy wren
and seeing life through the bleak.

Mind Time

I look out at the beach
as night begins to fall.
Echoes of a time still
splash in my ears.
It is persistent,
gently prying into the
silver moon of my mind,
where the tide has come
to shore and wallows.

Time lapses as I stare
at the swelling waves of the sea.
They do beckon me to visit,
to take the plunge into the
deep reefs below ...
my feelings.

Instead, I sit on the sand,
digging my feet in,
cooling myself down.

I remain at the shore,
my home,
wakeful heart alert
to the ever shifting waves ...
of my time.

Whispering Wind

Whispering wind,
a quiet breath
exhaled across years
of tiny, fragments of light.
Glowing in the breeze,
like silent fireworks,
accentuating my wanders
through life's debris.

Raw rustlings of leaves,
swaying gently in the wind,
soothe my spirit
and calm my busy mind.
I inhale as leaves rise
and exhale as they fall,
allowing myself to
exist in harmony
with the kinetic energy
of the whispering wind.

An ascending pathway
of spiralling wind,
encircles the aged,
thick trunks of trees
whose leaves
sway rhythmically
in the breeze.

It is a wind alight with
dots of dusty light.
Glowing attics of my privacy:
moments lived
and suspended in time.

Meditating, my palms
carry the dotted lights,
visualising their moments
and exhaling their negative energies
into the soothing,
accompanying breeze.

I am healed and at peace.

Ever Changing Rhythms of Life

My feet roam summer's vista,
saturated with greens and red.
Hues that glow alive with life,
inviting my story play outside.

A single note reveals its sound,
unravelling itself into the aether.
Drawn to its beginnings, I step,
adrift with its enticing tune.

Notes linger beneath my fingers,
waiting for their time to play.
I hold their energy, their zest,
their rhythms of life upon earth.

A butterfly flutters, adrift
with the gentle lilt of wind.
Its light, rhythmic wings
kiss the soft air lyrically.

Inspired, I turn now, slowly,
free moving with the rhythm.
Feeling the air upon my skin,
releasing notes into the air.

Scattering their sound among
nature's vibrant, rich finery.
The notes release their tune,
thriving with ideas anew.

A harmony fills my heart,
allowing my eyes to truly see.
Uplifted I am by such wonders,
cherishing their moments of life.

Moments that linger with me,
long after I wander my treks.
Presenting their symbols of life,
like the red-orange leaves of ...
remnance.

Leaves I twist between my fingers,
closing my eyes as thoughts drift.
Into the momentous winds of time,
the red-orange will soon afloat.

For Autumn hues are unravelling
through the waning summer days.
'Tis the season of yearning passion
and lyric to my heart and mind.

For Autumn reveals life's tunes
as inconstant and ever changing.
A terrain of vibrancy, yet danger,
as time reveals its very fragility.

So now I listen to the soaring wind
as it carries its gentle harmony.
Stepping towards autumn's lure,
I unravel the rhythms of life.

Spring's Touch

The budding delicacy of spring,
thrives with blossom and green.
A sensuous unfurling of white petals,
drizzled with the drops of fog's mist.

Fog's haze does saturate the air,
dressing us with a silver sheen.
An overhanging ruler of the light of day,
a shield to the radiance of the sun.

Bare and glistening blooms do reach,
longing to connect with my being.
Setting my feminine spirit alight
in a tightly wound body of darkness.

The promise of fortuitous fruit,
arouses my thirst to conquer
a world of madness and dark rule,
with womanhood as my stealth.

Raw and cascading blooms caress,
my receptive skin, which tingles alive.
No rules do my instincts follow now,
connected with the abundant flora.

Spring's Touch

The blossom's alluring scent prevails,
warding off the pending wrath of fog.
Enticed by its beauty, I submit myself
to the intoxicating scent of flora.

In sensuality, the control does lift,
its burdens released from my spirit.
No madness will dictate my journey
as I face the crossroads of my origin.

At peace with my spirit presently,
finding momentum in an old world.
Where blossom resides in shadows
of a desperate, wounded heart.

To anticipate the fruit of life,
unravelling itself through fog's tears.
To behold its unique way of being
as it blooms its ways through life.

A Writer's Company

Morning's canopy adrift with sail,
stream lining the cresting winds.
Outstretched, my body welcomes light,
which adorns the new year's day.

Bright blue and yellow pallets glow,
alluring me across nature's stream.
Treading afloat in an array of roses,
soft yellow petals awakening dreams.

So precious life afloat here now,
rustling gently across the breeze.
It takes one step for me to engage
with the gum's wisdom outreached.

Aboard a boat of leaves I float,
allowing new stories to unfold.
Of cresting and falling winds,
streaking words across the sky.

A Writer's Company

Years have passed since my life met,
the weather at sail beneath its soul.
Like nature I tread the ever changing,
my heart and mind open to all I face.

A writer's new buds can be unravelled
as they crest and fall across shifting winds.
Thoughts and words can reach out
across air's distance to all who read.

And so another path is revealed,
for me to unravel across the days.
Arms open I am soulful and willing,
to tread a writer's world with company.

My Beautiful Mother

I watch you walk
across the earth.
You are a gentle, peaceful view
in this very busy world.

You show me how to step
where you tread
and face the world
with a smile.

You help me play
in new lands
freely with
imagination.

Be it light and free
or busy with flight,
I want to do what
you do.

When you hold me close,
I breathe in your
special scent.
You are my sanctuary.

Take my hand
and show me
that the world
is not so big.

Teach me to do
the things you do.
To be the way
you are.

Our bond is unique,
we grow together.
Everyday and forever,
you are my
beautiful mother.

Pearl Melody

I wear the pearls of age
loosely around my wrist.
A reminder of my childhood,
they shake as I walk ...

At times the pearls will jump
off my wrist and jangle tunes
amongst the tiny buds of spring.
Celebratory melodies of new life.

A small patch of crimson carpet
lies deep within the grass.
A reminder of my regal duties,
which I wish to avoid today.

New blood is needed here
on the grounds of being.
I wear the rags of time kept,
disguising my rich ancestry.

If I stand on the red carpet
I can command my setting.
Immersing myself in new worlds,
whose varied lives I care for.

Amongst the people I walk,
opening my eyes wide to see,
what melodies are needed where,
so my pearls can work their magic.

For it is song that rings in time
as the tunes of life hum along.
Adding their own harmonies,
as they work out ways to be.

In my dreams the flowers bloom
into many happy human faces
who dance with me in the grass
and eat from shared food plates.

No title do I give my time,
as it would diminish melody.
Making it too deep a tune
with regal responsibility.

The pearls' melodies flow,
in the youthful breeze.
As the flowers begin to bloom
I wait to meet new human faces.

In this dream state I wish to stay
while tunes continue to ring.
I will compose my own lyrics
as I find my own life rhythm.

Letter Jumble

I crawl carefully underneath
a stack of notes piled high.
Lines waiting for my ears
to hear the word rhythm.

Single letters scrape against
bare paper as it flutters.
Sharp and tall they reach
for a whole word existence.

My hands ache from grasping
metal and wooden stencils,
from which I cut out letters
some large, some very small.

The letters group and swing
to beats against the floor,
as I press my feet down hard
upon the wooden floor boards.

The words will not form
in these large brick walls.
They need fresh air outside
to breathe and truly play.
I am nearly standing now
and should really go
through that door ...

There is the coat stand,
jazzing away in the corner.
Swinging your coat around
and chuckling with laughter.

Your pockets are full of letters,
which you jumbled in a mess.
Trying to explain your thoughts,
leaving a word trail of ...
meaning.

I will find your words
playing outside in the sun.
They will drift in the breeze
and hide away from storms.
They'll be comforting
in your own way ...

I am now standing up
and grabbing my coat again.
Letter filled pockets sigh
as I slip my arms inside.

My old, heavy grey coat,
carrying my letter jumble
outside ...
to meet you.

Trekking an Age of Light

The dark shifts across the terrain,
its shadows casting soft images
of silhouettes against the night sky.
Their presence warms my heart
and I extend my arm into the aether.

The wind blows across my skin
in small, gentle gusts of energy.
Its touch, its presence, I feel
as I connect with spirits of an age
that existed long before I breathed
my very presence upon this terrain.

Presently, time does freeze,
capturing a moment of silence.
Shifting silhouettes reach across
the age of wise, ticking time towards
my present being and all it is.

Dressed in white, embodying all ages,
I am a figure of a people who lit their way,
across the dark of night into light's hope.
Right here, right now, I embody
the lasting energy of a people's heritage.

Striking a sulfur match against the fence,
I watch the flame spark its fiery life.
My arm shakes with anxiety.
I hold one very last tallow candle,
an object of great, human desire.

The silhouettes lean towards me,
their voices hoarse whispers
that coast across the night air.
Long live the tallow! They chant.
Bring back our light of life!

Fingers shaking, I hold the candle,
setting wick alight with orange spark.
As the flame glows across the black,
it reveals the warm flesh of faces.
Eyes shine wide with soaring hope,
mouths fall open with anticipation.

The world unravels itself before me,
revealing an age of desired light.
I step gently across the terrain,
passing through a wave of silhouettes
who shift aside to let me see.

Windows do glow with soft candlelight,
as do the streets with rush lights aglow.
Yet the sound of screaming masks the peace,
as a people shout their heartfelt protests.
For some windows are dark, eerie and silent,
awaiting the wash of light to thrive.

Holding the burning tallow in the air,
I watch the orange-yellow sparks fly.
A loyal message I release into the night
and watch it dazzle through dark's cloak,
passing its way through ages of time.

Dusk Heart

Dusk whispers softly,
soothing day's roaring reds.
I let dusk enter my heart,
flickering soft purple wishes.

I could follow dusk always,
brushing it with stripes and dots
of simple beginnings
for us to share in time.

We could walk in dusk's glow,
basking in the purple gleam.
Letting our hearts share dreams
of the journeys we are yet to face.

For in this light no mile is far,
more a simple glance ahead.
The horizon seems very close,
we could reach it quickly together.

Let dusk allow our hearts to dream
and love our time away,
from the fiery reds of life
that swelter during bright daylight.

Bare Desire

Dusk's energy hums
with electric life,
vibrating under my
warm, receptive skin.
A song of street life
as day's worries pass,
stirring my shadowed soul
with renewed promise.
I search for you.

A crazy crowd
presses on.
Strangers push passed
my solo self,
entranced by night's
soaked sounds
and visual vibrancy.

A mesmerising melody
arises from the asphalt.
The sultry, still heat
shifts into a soft,
airy breeze.

Sensually, I move,
absorbing dusk's energy.
Feeling its deep hum
vibrate within
the very depths
of my seeking soul.
I am burning for you.

My feet are light,
lifting my weight
as I spin slowly,
unravelling myself
like an untangled ribbon.

Bare, naked light
radiates from me.
Neon lights aglow,
an array of colours
that pulse with the heat
of summer's swelter.

Your light appears,
a throbbing glow
that stirs my soul.
Your deep, intense eyes
gaze straight into mine,
ablazing my light
with a fiery flame.

Shifting closer
you move with me,
your hips grinding
against mine.
Shirt unbuttoned,
bare chest taught
and strikingly beautiful.

Sensually sexy, you are,
your confident composure
arresting my aroused self.
My dreams have drifted
above the streets,
calling your name,
willing you to
melt in my
flaming femininity.

Your liquid voice
caresses my soul.
It seeps through the cracks
of day's wrath
that I have clung to
so tightly.
It fills my heart
with hope.

Neon lights aflame,
I pulse with passion,
my spirit soaring
as your lips
press against mine.

Sheer ecstasy reigns,
lifting us above
the streets.
Our spirit lights
are drawn together
like magnets.

The world below mutes,
caught in its grind.
Time slows as
we rise higher.

I melt in your glow,
stripping myself bare,
showing myself to you.
Your burning lips
arouse me deeply.
We are united,
our hot heat
radiating across
the sultry sky.

I surrender myself
to you,
crying out in climax,
my soul radiating
with ecstasy.

Soaring through the dark,
our lights burn brightly,
blending their colours
into new, promising shades.

We are connecting,
raw with passion.
Embracing, we sink
into summer's sultry night,
surrendering once more
to our burning desires.

Kite Day

The kite soars
high in the sky.
A myriad of colours
gliding by ...
day swept.

This is our day
to see each other.
Morning air holds hope
of losing real time
and escaping into...
colour land.

We could shimmer
like a goldfish in water.
Glide like a purple dotted
aeroplane through
low silver cloud.

Watch the colourful world
unfold from way up high.
Enjoying the lapse
of kite day time.

As the day sweep
winds to an end,
let's descend gently
and ease back into ...
real time.

New Clay Linen

White linen presses against my skin,
cooling my mind this long, warm day.
It is a new dress I choose to wear,
spinning around the summer jetty.

The wood planks are rough and firm
beneath my very bare, sore feet.
I spin until reaching the water's edge,
white linen wrapping around me.

Across the sea, the lighthouse beckons,
emitting its light over a ship wreck.
A past danger I witnessed days ago
while circling the lighthouse tower.

I abandoned the ship wreck out at sea,
where it continues to scream and kick.
Each night I fall into a restless sleep,
nightmares of fleeing haunting me.

On this jetty I feel calm and safe,
free from the dark mass at sea.
Walking circles around wooden planks,
I wait for you to come and join me.

It may be a long time before you arrive.
Have you managed to escape like me?
I fled away behind the sharp rocks,
angry sailor voices chasing after me.

We must continue to run and hide
as angry fingers point in our direction.
Stern sailors continue to seek us out,
hoping to claim their treasure back.

It was dark that night with little starlight,
as we peered behind the lighthouse tower.
We spotted a large ship decked with chests,
evidently filled with discovered treasure.

We crawled in closer to see the loot,
eyes wide with sheer excitement and glee.
To think that we had spotted a pirate ship,
floating in the deep waters of the sea.

Hooded figures jumped upon the deck,
torch lights flashing to see their way.
Raised voices and strength erupted
in a volcanic explosion of attack.

Huddled together in the grainy sand,
we could not shift our gaze away.
We watched as treasures were looted
by the hooded figures who ran away.

Minutes later we were discovered
by sailors searching for their looters.
Huddled together in the grainy sand,
we were frisked for stolen treasure.

I choose to hide in my white linen,
posing as an every day civilian.
The lighthouse's light still beckons to me:
You know that I am reaching for you!

The lighthouse's light flickers its rays,
across the jetty ground I stand upon.
Light continues to bounce off the sand,
I shaped earlier in heaps with my hands.

Like clay was the sand in my fingers,
moulding into hooded, echoing figures.
Past clay voices mixed with sea water,
gurgling words of anger and blame.

I now smear sand clay upon my dress,
white linen heavy with new marks.
I carry the harsh voices as I spin around
and open my arms to the lighthouse.

You'll find me here upon the jetty,
newly dressed in clay white linen.
Your echoing voices a mere thought
as I refuse to accept the blame.

The sandy clay figures do sigh
as they face the turn of the tide.
It washes away their very existence,
leaving me to face the long trek back.

Back to the lighthouse I will return,
disguised in new clay white linen.
I know you shine a light in the tower,
reaching for me across the dark sea.

Atlas' Groove

After day, a dust rises,
tiny granules land
on my bare skin.
So stark is my breath,
a soul's whisper that
stirs my feelings within.

Atlas' groove remains,
grounding its rhythm
as I dig my heels deep.
Remnant heat of day,
still hot to touch,
jolts me wide awake.

In sand knee high,
I still my mind
against the force of tide,
enclosing itself upon me.
To remain fixed and alert,
in a land unfamiliar,
is truly no mean feat.

Rhythmic dreams unravel
in my disoriented mind.
Symphonies of feverish sleep,
echoing with Atlas' treks
and alluring visions.

In night, fire sparks,
distant, yet near,
beckoning to me.
A dangerous cloak,
smothering eve's silence
with the will of metal.

We look to the sky,
in search of fortune
as our feet bleed
across Atlas' traps.

In deep dug holes,
a lingering groove
voices the wisdom
of its adventurer.

Piles of sand seep
between finger gaps,
releasing echoes of
lives once present here.
This shore, a rhythm
of arrivals and departures,
of spirits who tried
to make their ways here.

Still, this atlas breathes,
amidst the loss and sparks,
a world that ebbs
and seeks its flow.
Its paths unclear,
yet set in time
at traveller's will.

Amongst debris
of day's forgets,
Atlas' map will
unravel itself.

In patches of land,
exposed with truth,
the soul will begin to fly.

In darkness resides
the core of life
and its manifestations.
In dreams awake,
the spirit soars,
seeking a place
to finally be.

Granules of danger,
I collect now in
the palm of my hand.
Tiny particles
that have carried
the trek of anger
across the land.

I yearn to hitch a ride,
cutting through the
dangerous web
of Atlas' deep secrets.

I will defeat the mind
that withholds the key
to desired justice
and a better life for all.

Warrior Spirit

Winter's snow falls white,
cooling the fire flowers
aflame across the forest floor.
Red-orange embers float
like paper pieces through air,
carrying secretly shared messages
across the burnt, buried city.

My booted feet land
on snow's white blanket.
Silent, solitary footsteps
carry me across the floor.

Red gold embers of fire
spark around my body,
singeing my skin on contact.
A body spent the wrath of death.

Extinguishing flame in ice cold,
I watch stinging scars form.
Standing solo under sheer white,
my ragged breath is iced.
I am as frozen as the death
that plagues my waking.
I am all who remains of my tribe.

Metal clangs and clashes,
stomping across snow.
Turning swiftly, I gaze
into blazing blue eyes.

A tribal tune unravels itself
under my singed skin,
stirring my severed soul.
Around me, chokes the breaths
of my own native city.
Severed bodies are scattered carelessly,
staring lifelessly at sky.
Victims of sinful slaughter
by a merciless, murdering clan.

Retrieving my sharp sword,
I clutch it very tightly,
maintaining determined eye contact
with the menacing man that I face.
I will not die here.

My sword's blade is sharp,
cutting through the air
and marking it with letters: *Ri* -

His rough hand grasps my wrist
holding my sword silent.
My still blade gleams
in the wintry white snowfall.

My blazing, beating heart
sets my willful eyes afire.
"I am here to -" I speak stubbornly
to the traitor, the defected,
who has betrayed us all.

My words drift off at the sight
of his sharp, striking features.
A familiar face whose atlas
I can trace in my dreams.

Ripping ragefully away,
my sword slices his hand.
Drops of blood drizzle
across the watchful white.
"Aagh!" He cries in pain,
grasping his gory wound.

Wildly, he reaches for me,
his eyes crazed and confused.
Grasping his gruesome sword,
he points it directly at me,
gasping to catch a breath.

Time sparks silently,
red flames flickering and fading,
wind sailing and falling,
hearts rising and sinking.

Summoning my energy,
I silence my inner screaming.
Twirling amongst the sparks,
I lift the hem of my skirt,
welcoming raw air onto my skin.
Awakening my warrior spirit,
I grasp my sword firmly in one hand.

Rikati. I wince as my skin severs
while I cut the loving letters
of my natal name into my leg's skin.
Blood drips down onto white,
marking my presence here.

I am Rikati of the Hirgo Tribe,
unafraid of you, traitor, Widago.
I will die adorned with my name
in memory of my loving people.

Widago's sword's blow
sends me flying backwards.
Staring up, I see his face,
sparking rageful red embers.
He carries the weight of life lost,
it eats away at his severed soul.

Manic moments pass as he stares,
blue eyes ablaze with inner conflict.
The steady white snow persists,
piling its pure white onto his armour.
Gradually, it simmers down his rage,
his gaze tormented as he meets
my hardened, awakened eyes.

Dramatically, Widago drops his sword,
marking his place in the wintry white snow.
Bowing in defeat, he walks away.

Flying Free

Atop a tall mountain ledge,
gazing at snow white clouds
circling surrounding tree tops.
A soft mist drizzles its drops
across my receptively warm skin.
Saturating self in surroundings,
auras awakening my tired spirit.

Rich, raw colour is a symphony,
shades of grey and blue
hum lyrically across the range.
Their colours stretching like light
that flows through the air,
unravelling its own pathway.

Atmospheric nature calls to me,
its rhythms acute and alive.
The sun's chant sounds as it peeks
through the cotton-like clouds,
mesmerising me with its healing light.

Stretching my arms out wide,
I absorb the sun's radiant energy
and my soul soars very high.
I am flying freely like a bird,
fluttering my feathered wings,
which beat with renewed hope.

Mind's fog begins to lift,
grey clouds shedding rain.
Worries that pitter patter
their essences across the range.
Up high I watch them dissipate,
blending in with the grey blue light.
A vista of vivescence gleams
as the light bounces off rocks and leaves.

Closing my eyes, I inhale
and exhale very gently.
In the darkness, I can still see ...
grey, blue and white lights aglow,
swarming in a saturated blend.
An amber-rose light emerges,
glowing its gentle warmth
and soothing my aching heart.

The sound of my beating wings
alerts me to my serene surroundings.
Opening my eyes, I harness my flight,
soaring serene loops through the air.
The warmth of the sun reassures me
that all will be okay in my world.

Dropping slowly, I begin to descend,
gravitating towards the mountain ledge.
As I land, I attune myself to my bare feet
standing on a smooth curve of rock.

A warmth alights my soul
and I exhale relief.
Gazing at my world, I admire its nature,
a place of rejuvenation and healing.
I am present and alive,
blessed with clarity of mind.

Evergold Dream
A Romantic and Poetic Tale

About Evergold Dream

*"Close your eyes and journey
into the world of golden lure.
Its path a light for the heart
to play in a new world breeze."*

Waking beneath the tree canopy one morning,
Bethany and Sibra discover a gold leaf.
Bethany is lured by it and shares her most fervent dream.

Soon after, Bethany has disappeared
from their loving home in the forest green
and is drifting in the world of golden leaves.

Determined to have his wife return,
Sibra faces the wild mountain,
which reveals her true desires …

Part 1

A golden hue streaks its light,
through the canopy of eve.
Its glow an enticing lure
for a very fervent dreamer.

Upon my shoulder sits a firefly,
who can see through gold's entice.
Shining a light upon one's truth,
it cuts to the very heart of a dream.

Gold leaves flutter in the air,
circling us as we try to navigate
our way across untravelled path,
searching for her single dream.

My fingers reach into my pocket,
feeling for the small gold leaf.
It floated passed us one morning
as we wakened beneath tree canopy.

Her green eyes were filled with joy
as she silently gave words to her dream.
As she reached for my embrace,
the gold leaf rested upon her cheek.

As time passed, the dream consumed her,
shifting her a great distance away.
She'd merely glance at the life we knew
in our modest home in the forest green.

I took the gold leaf one morning
from her clenched hand as she slept.
She lay outside on the pine needle floor
in front of the home we had made.

It is her desire I dare to discover
within this golden world of lure.
I hope to see her smiling eyes,
to feel her familiar embrace.

Gold leaves lift us up high above
the wide canopy of trees below.
They whisper that her desired dream,
thrives within a silvery mountain peak.

The firefly flutters ahead of me,
flickering light upon the rock base.
Here my feet do firmly land,
once golden leaves release me.

A blast of cold air hits me hard,
stumbling me flat upon the rock.
Struggling to my feet, I stand,
my gaze falling upon my destination.

The silvery peak is way up high,
a challenge for a person to reach.
It houses her pure dream desire,
which one needs bravery to face.

The firefly reads my tired state
and leads me across the rock surface.
Weathering rock reveals itself,
creating a void that's large and dark.

Following the firefly through the void,
we stumble across a modest cave.
It is big enough to lie in tonight
and shelter us from the blasting wind.

The firefly's light casts a bright glow,
warming me in the cold, dark cave.
Lying down, I let my eyes droop,
clutching her gold leaf as I sleep.

Part 2

As morning wakes, my eyes open,
adjusting to the new white light.
Standing, I stretch and walk,
taking in the wondrous sights.

Intricate cave art has been etched
upon the very tall, rocky walls.
It tells tales of journeys taken
by those who travelled this far.

They arrived on golden leaves,
floating through the light air.
Catching the drift beneath them,
enticed by the lure of gold.

The gold leaves seem to play,
tossing and shifting in the breeze.
Binding their bright golden hues
around innocent travellers' heads.

Staring at the gold leaf in my hand,
I consider the power it exudes.
Enticing one with gold's promise,
while manipulating their dreams.

One gold leaf has consumed her,
my beautiful, charming wife.
It has estranged her from me,
her heart feeling unfulfilled.

Her arms no longer reached for me,
as the night fell upon day.
Her bright green eyes dimmed,
shutting out her joyful way.

How I long to reach her
and rediscover our love again.
I will bring her back home to me,
going wherever she wishes to be.

The firefly has left the cave,
journeying out into the light.
Stepping outside, I inhale a breath,
as I witness the amazing sights.

Carpeted along the rock face
is a village of honeycomb houses,
within which live many a bee,
buzzing and playing freely.

The buzz echoes across the rocks,
bouncing out into the open air.
It takes on a familiar rhythm,
I have heard in my wake before.

Once my wife stood inside our home,
clutching a bunch of gardenias.
She sang the very same tune,
arranging the flowers in a vase:

"Close your eyes and journey
into the world of golden lure.
Its path a light for the heart
to play in a new world breeze."

The tune was with us while I cupped
her beautiful face in my hands.
As we lay down by the open fire,
I felt her struggle in my embrace.

She could no longer meet my eyes
with her striking green gaze.
Her mind was drifting elsewhere,
to a new and different place.

As my memory slowly fades,
I feel my knees begin to shake.
I wonder what I am to do
upon this very mountain ledge.

The firefly greets me happily,
sharing with me some honey.
The bees had welcomed it inside
their homes that very morning.

The honey is a golden brown
and very rich in flavour.
I savour every last drop,
my head beginning to spin.

I feel a strange sensation
fluttering across my skin.
It is like thousands of fireflies
are flapping their wings.

Suddenly I can really hear
the voices of the bees.
I understand their language
as they speak freely to me.

The bees share more honey,
feeding us both until we're full.
I practice my new bee language
as I listen to their mountain stories.

The bees warn us not to travel
upon the steep mountain slope.
It is dangerous gold leaf territory,
seducing many a restless traveller.

We're told dreams lose their owner
and belong to the golden leaves.
The owner wanders empty
and searching for a way to be.

I consider my wife's dulled eyes,
her endless, searching nature.
I fear her dream has been snatched,
leaving her roaming and empty.

At the end of the meal we thank
the bees for their hospitality.
They offer to fly us up higher
towards the silvery mountain peak.

Surrounded by hundreds of bees,
we are gently flown upwards.
We land upon a new ledge
decorated with blueberry trees.

The trees hang precariously
off the sides of several rocks.
The blueberries dangle freely,
abundant and food aplenty.

The bees share some more honey
before they leave us be.
They tell us we are safe here
beneath the blueberry trees.

As the sun begins to fade,
the firefly's light glows.
It shares with me its discovery
of the golden leaf's mission.

Evergold Dream

It had visited the gold leaf territory,
upon the steep mountain slope.
Buzzing in the air it hovered,
watching as a world unfolded.

The gold leaves were replaying
images from human dreams.
Pausing and rewinding images
and manipulating precious moments.

I consider my wife's lyrics,
sung so clearly to me that night:
Its path a light for the heart
to play in a new world breeze.

The song began to make sense
and so did my wife's fate.
In this land of evergold dreams
I will fight to save her being.

Part 3

I am met with a foggy mist
in a vivid waking dream.
Eyelids fluttering open slowly,
I see her in her beauty.

The blueberry trees have grown
much taller than last evening.
They soar high into the sky,
swinging a hum in the wind.

Her back is standing to me,
her long black hair flowing.
She carries her weaved basket,
picking giant, fresh blueberries.

The hum is intoxicating,
evoking memories of times,
I slow danced with her outside
our home in the forest green.

We would sweep across the plain,
laughing as we stumbled.
Arms around each other tightly,
hearts beating our special rhythm.

There she is now flowing
in a gentle, musical breeze.
She sets the full basket down
and stretches her arms freely.

Standing, I approach my wife,
still feeling groggy in the mist.
I can only take a few steps
before the boundary kicks in.

She is in a separate world,
one I cannot even reach.
She turns around and I see
how tired she really is.

My wife wears the lines of fatigue
upon her eyes and brow.
Her expression is of sadness
as she absorbs her world.

The wild mountainside sways,
creaking loudly in the wind.
The air blast hits her sharply,
landing her upon the rock.

She rolls upon her side
and pulls herself to her feet.
Dashing through the wind gusts,
she shelters under blueberry trees.

My wife shakes in the wind,
cold and weak at once.
I wish I could reach her
and wrap her in my warmth.

I feel a flutter on my shoulder,
it is my friend the firefly.
It is glowing brightly
with a very warm heat.

It crosses into my wife's dream,
warming the blasting air.
Setting the foggy mist aglow
with yellow-orange light.

The mist dissipates to warmth
and the wind ceases blasting.
All that can be heard is crackling
like the sound of an open fire.

The warmth hugs her gently,
ridding the mountain of its chill.
Relaxing, she allows herself to sit
upon the grassy green surround.

I stand in tremendous awe
of the firefly's abilities
to comfort my wife with warmth
in this vivid mountain dream.

The firefly grabs a blueberry
from the harvest in the basket.
It carries it in its tiny legs,
fluttering through the air.

The blueberry turns orange,
aglow with the warmth of light.
It shines in the air as the firefly,
glides gently to my wife's side.

The new orange berry catches
the attention of her gaze.
Reaching into the air slowly,
she lets it land into her palm.

As she eats the orange berry,
my wife's face forms a smile.
Her fatigue seems to disappear,
core strength is returning now.

My wife searches for the giver
of the orange berry magic.
The firefly has already vanished
from her vivid mountain dream.

As the firefly returns to me,
I thank it with my eyes.
It rests gently on my shoulder,
my friend through this plight.

I stay staring at her infinitum,
refusing to leave her dream side.
Upon this mountain dream,
sits my very beautiful wife.

Reaching into my pocket,
I hold the gold leaf gently.
My wife's evergold dream
has consumed her in its world.

Part 4

My wife has been busy gathering.
The blueberries are all harvested
and are a glossy blue in her basket.
She places a handful at the boundary.

"Sibra?" She mouths my name softly.
Peering through the boundary,
her hand shields her eyes from the sun.
Alas, she cannot see me at all.

I step forward, wanting to hold her,
to take her away from this place.
I cannot cross over the boundary.
We remain at a distance, like strangers.

Setting my sights on a blueberry,
I bend down and stretch out my hand.
Flexing and grasping at the fruit
until it flicks up into my palm.

I am amazed we have connected.
Tears spring to my eyes and I weep.
My wife knows I am here with her.
The mountain scape is renewed with hope.

My wife has fallen to her knees.
"My loving husband, Sibra," she sobs.
Tears stream down her cheeks.
"I knew you were here with me."

"My beautiful Bethany, I am always here,"
I am still weeping with gratitude.
She hears my voice and smiles,
her eyes shining with love and hope.

"I can't see you, my dear Sibra,"
Bethany wipes away at her tears.
"I know you can see me though."
She rests her hand on her heart.

"Yes, I can," I say very gently.
"I miss you with all my heart."
I can't take my eyes off her.
"I miss you too, Sibra," she sighs.

The breeze picks up suddenly,
blowing at us in gentle gusts.
A familiar mint green dances gently,
floating through the breeze.

Mint green leaves like those on trees
outside the front door of our home.
The leaves that fell upon us gently,
the day I proposed to my Bethany.

The mint green leaves rustle gently,
swirling in the air around my wife.
A choppy breeze, like seawater,
makes the leaves rise and fall.

Bethany is nauseas, I can tell.
Her lips are clamped together.
One hand lies across her stomach
and her body leans against a trunk.

Vertigo has crept its way here,
dizzying the blueberry serenity.
Electric lightening strikes its path,
jolting her into alert wakefulness.

The mint leaves multiply in number,
bursting through gusts of wind.
They rise to the height of wave peaks,
transporting Bethany through the air.

She is bobbing in mint green sea,
sweeping across the mountain scape.
Looking down at the gold leaf world,
closing her eyes and finding strength.

Her determination fills my heart
with undying love for my wife.
I can see she is fighting to keep
the strength of her awakened self.

Alighting and surfing the leaves,
she rides them through the breeze.
Across the steep cliffs she travels,
collecting more mint green leaves.

Raising her hand, Bethany waves,
conducting the leaves to create.
Subsiding, the waves break down,
forming an image of a small house.

It is a house made of cedar wood,
felled from surrounding forest green.
A heavy wooden door swings open,
revealing the view of the hallway.

Across this threshold I carried my wife,
the day she married me under trees.
Our hearts danced together as one
in our loving home in the forest green.

Bethany floats into the hallway,
a trail of leaves close behind her.
Gathering a piece of parchment,
she searches for a writing tool.

The straw flower she once arranged
is plucked from its ornate vase.
Using its stem, she writes a note,
releasing the parchment into the air.

The parchment floats very slowly
through the much calmer breeze.
Falling and falling it finally lands
at my feet on the mountainside.

Bending down I gently collect
the fluttering white parchment.
It rests gently in both my hands,
revealing Bethany's short message:

*Follow me across the mountain
into our mint green lives.
My dream will stay awake
if I remember our times.*

Looking up, I watch my dear Bethany,
warming herself by the cosy fire.
She is immersing herself in memories
of our loving home in the forest green.

Part 5

The first snow falls heavily
upon the mountainside.
It is winter here in isolation,
a time to seek better refuge.

A snow line has begun to form
upon this windward slope.
As the snow falls, it extends,
creating a slippery ground to cross.

Standing upon a large rock slab,
I look down where Bethany resides.
She is sitting on the snow line path,
catching a snow crystal in her palms.

Mint green leaves remain in her hair,
dotted with the white of snow fall.
Her eyes shine brightly in the cold,
enchanted with the beauty that unfolds.

The snow crystal is a stellar dendrite,
its six arms symmetrically beautiful.
Even in heavy snow it glistens,
a bright light in the snow storm.

The heavy snow ceases its cascade,
highlighting a moment of still life.
The mint leaves land on each dendrite arm
and the land transforms itself once more.

The snow line is the one we played on
outside our home one morning.
There is the snow man we created,
with two large stones for its eyes.

The snow man has gained a voice,
which it uses to whisper a warning:
"Gold leaves wait up ahead for you,
wishing to destroy your precious memory."

"Sibra?" Bethany sounds afraid.
I descend the rock slab to the snow line.
Standing at the boundary's edge,
I stare at my dear wife.

She has placed the snowflake in her pocket
and it begins to drip as it melts.
"Time is short, keep playing," I say,
hoping to keep her dream alive.

"I see," Bethany stands tall and runs,
hiding behind the snow man.
"Come get me Sibra," she calls.
"Like you did once before."

I feel the firefly warming up
inside my thick winter coat.
It flickers, motioning for me
to step into Bethany's world.

I feel light, like a soft memory
floating slowly into the scene.
Approaching the snow man, I smile
at the beautiful face of my wife.

"I see you flickering before me, Sibra,"
Bethany reaches out to touch me.
I do not feel her hand upon me,
a mere image I am in her memory.

Bethany's face falls in sadness
as she realises we are still distanced.
I am pleased enough to be next to her,
sharing in our life memory together.

Following Bethany around the snowman,
I feel the wind blowing me around.
I am as light as paper in this moment,
like a printed photograph in an album.

I can feel the very luscious snow,
crunching softly beneath my feet.
I can hear Bethany's excited laughter,
as she forms a snow ball in her hands.

"Watch out Sibra!" Bethany laughs.
Looking up I see her face lit up
as she bites her tongue in concentration.
Raising her arms, she throws the snowball …

It vanishes completely in mid air.
Bethany's mouth drops open,
her hands begin to shake.
"Sibra?" She is suddenly afraid.

Airborne snow particles surround us,
raised by the wind into the air.
The blowing snow reaches a great height,
making it very hard to see each other.

Flickering images we are in the snow,
flashing through a blind, cold fog.
Reaching out for each other's light,
unable to navigate through vast white.

"Sibra!" Bethany shouts my name,
I can hear her soft voice shaking.
"Keep calm," I call back gently.
"Ignore this part of your dream."

I cannot see my beautiful wife,
behind the thick screen of snow.
I do hear her silence in the white,
as she reflects upon her memory.

The snow blows over the edge
of the cliff we both drift upon.
In seconds the snow accumulates
over hanging the cliff in a cornice shape.

The normality of time is changed here,
minutes transformed into mere seconds.
It is a sign the gold leaves have found us
and are controlling Bethany's memory.

The wind blown snow falls more heavily,
striking my body, face and head.
Pushing through strong blasts, I move
towards the overhanging cliff cornice.

Upon the cornice I crouch and peer,
at the world lying below the cliff.
I am faced with the serene calmness
of a grassy valley on a sunny day.

Looking up, I see the rich blue
of the ever reaching, endless sky.
The silvery peak shines brightly,
a reminder of Bethany's desires.

"Where are you Sibra?" Bethany calls,
her voice frightened and unsure.
"Over here!" I call back loudly.
"Follow the sound of my voice."

Fresh fallen snow and winds persist,
accumulating in snowdrift masses.
It is a challenge to press on through
the very thick blasts of snowfall.

I continue to call Bethany's name,
trying to see her through the haze.
Her voice is faint in response,
buried within the snow's icy blasts.

Bending down in the snowy mass,
I pick up a handful of glossy white.
Cupping cold snow in both hands,
I stand very still and close my eyes.

Pure soft snow, you are here with us,
allowing us to revel in a memory.
Please carry us within your drift,
up high towards the mountain peak.

Slowly I rise into the air,
my body light and drifting.
My gaze rests upon Bethany
who is also rising gracefully.

Relief forms upon her face
and she raises her arms up high.
The snow storm gently eases,
replaced by floating snow flakes.

Like stars alight are the snowflakes,
guiding our path across the sky.
Together we are journeying,
fighting to keep her dream alive.

Bethany floats towards me
and reaches for my hands.
Clutching her fingers, I weep,
blessed with her love and warmth.

Part 6

An age passes as we rise,
the cold air stinging our skins.
A light wind blows its rhythm
with the fluttering of golden leaves.

Circling around us wildly,
the leaves shaken poor Bethany.
No words I speak as I tighten
my grasp of her trembling hands.

My eyes locked with hers, I smile,
empowering her with the will to be.
In our bond she has found comfort
in the rhythm existing between us.

The gold leaves cling to Bethany's arms,
offering to give her flight ahead.
I watch as my wife's eyes glaze over,
enticed by the strong lure of gold.

A tormented heart beats in my wife,
wrestling with her will to be.
The leaves pull at her body sharply,
loosening her grip of my hands.

Bethany is fading away from our now,
retreating back into the golden world.
Shaking her head she chooses to fight
and grasps my fingers very tightly.

As the leaves pull more sharply, she gasps,
attempting to shake them from her body.
They do not relent, yet drag her firmly,
releasing her right hand from my grasp.

"Sibra!" Bethany cries loudly,
her body is shaking with fear.
Her left hand grips mine firmly
as she struggles against gold's grasp.

"Look at me, Bethany," I say,
settling the storm of her struggle.
My gaze meeting hers, I will her to be,
to focus on our very connection.

In both our hands, our spirits lie,
facing our wrath with raw will.
Drawing Bethany close, I sigh,
our hearts beating a special rhythm.

Bound together, our bodies wrap,
entwined in a moment of deep love.
Together we both begin to fall,
descending stormy, leaf swept aether.

Our feet soon land upon the silver
of the ethereal mountain peak.
In darkness, the firefly alights,
revealing a leaf littered pathway.

Monochromatic leaves, which sit,
awaiting the voice of Bethany's dream.
A desire that engulfs her heart
and wrestles with her living spirit.

The gold leaves pull at Bethany's hair,
attempting to drag her away.
She stamps her foot strongly,
freezing the gold leaf in motion.

Bethany meets my worried gaze
with her gentle, loving eyes.
Placing one hand on my cheek,
she smiles gently before speaking.

"My true desire, my loving Sibra,
is to journey much further away.
Beyond the mountain, no gold awaits
and our mint green lives will play."

The monochromatic leaves do shake,
releasing a single, mint green leaf.
It floats lightly through the air
and lands in Bethany's open palm.

The gold leaves release Bethany,
shattering into tiny pieces.
Picked up by the wind they sail,
into the distant, unknown aether.

Shifting my gaze, I stare at mint green,
enchanted by its pure, delicate life.
A treasure to behold in this moment
of precious, soulful connection.

My heart beats strongly as I meet,
the hopeful gaze of my wife.
Extending my hand, I accept
the delicate, mint green leaf.

What love and home I do behold,
within the grasp of my hand.
My words come to me naturally,
as I feel the energy of mint green:

"Travel with you, I will,
across our mint green lives.
Together we will only grow
and embrace our time."

Bethany's eyes shed happy tears
and she steps into my embrace.
Holding her closely, I exhale,
relieved to have her return to me.

Above us, a snowflake does shine,
sharing its unique, delicate wisdom.
It speaks of an age of discovery
of our newfound steps together.

About the Author

Susan Marshall is a novelist, fiction writer, poet, dramatist and essayist and the founder of Story Playscapes. She is also a theatre practitioner and an expert educator. Susan is highly skilled in working with young adults in theatrical, educational and community settings and is a recipient of a prestigious award for her outstanding and extensive work with young people.

Susan's love for the arts began in early childhood. She discovered she had a strong physical connection with her surroundings (her playscapes) and could work with moments of energetic motions, letting them breathe and take flight through writing and performance work. She has fond memories of her parents encouraging her to read and write stories. She would also decorate her backyard with sheets as curtains and invite her parents as audience members to share in her performance work.

Susan's first productions were in primary school, under the experienced guidance of her significant teachers: Kim Young and Stu Cooper. She portrayed the Narrator in the stage adaptation of Road Dahl's *James and the Giant Peach*. In her French studies, she also had the fortune to portray the King in the French stage adaptation of *Le Petit Prince* by Antoine de Saint-Exupéry.

In secondary school, Susan felt blessed to be taught English and Drama by Di Gagen, the professional Australian theatre critic and stage director. Di was instrumental in helping Susan to discover and harness her artistic nature and skills. Under Di's guidance, Susan learnt how to critique live theatrical performance and to further develop and refine her writing skills.

Di Gagen also trained Susan in the art of theatre direction, by allowing her to take on the role of Stage Director for the productions: *Just Equal* by Dennis Betts and *A Midsummer Night's Dream* by William Shakespeare. Susan also had the privilege of being taught the skills of professional pantomimic performance when she was cast as various roles, including Phoebe and a Field Mouse in A. A. Milne's *Toad of Toad Hall*, which was co-directed by Di and Steve Gagen at the Hartwell Players in Melbourne.

Di Gagen also introduced Susan to the world of St Martin's Youth Arts Centre in Melbourne. Susan spent many years there, further developing her skills in performance. She was privileged to be trained in the techniques of improvisation by the experienced Geoff Wallis and even participated in a number of *Theatresports* regional finals.

Another highlight for Susan at St Martin's Youth Arts Centre, was the opportunity to be trained by the professional actor, James Wardlaw, in Stanislavski's method acting techniques. Susan also worked closely with the highly esteemed Artistic Director, Brett Adam, on devising and writing the script for the production of *Orb.IT* for the Melbourne International Arts Festival. As an actor, Susan also enjoyed portraying various roles in the non-realistic production within the modern set design created by Darryl Cordell.

Susan attended La Trobe University, where she completed a Bachelor of Arts and majored in English and Theatre and Drama. In her English degree, she committed herself to learning to read, analyse and write a range of narrative types, from classical to post structuralist. Professor Richard Freadman was a significant lecturer for Susan, due to his encouragement of her reading and analysis skills in autobiographical texts; along with broadening her understandings of the notions of the self in writing and literary theory.

In her Theatre and Drama degree, Susan was fortunate to be taught the art of theatre performance and theory by the highly experienced and esteemed, late Geoffrey Milne. She was also blessed to learn from the amazing expertise of the theatre practitioners: Julian Meyrick, Peta Tait and Meredith Rogers.

At La Trobe University, Susan also enjoyed portraying various roles in the theatrical production: *As You Like It*, by William Shakespeare, directed by Meredith Rogers and performed at the Trades Hall in Melbourne. She also performed the protagonist in the post structuralist production of Virginia Baxter's *What Time is This House?* at the Melbourne Fringe Festival. Later, she performed Phrygenia in the production *Spartacus and Phrygenia*, (written and directed by Peter and Corinne at Créations Barquette Gitane), for the Banyule Festival in Melbourne.

Keen to learn more about theatre direction, Susan had the privilege of observing and being taught by the professional stage director, Richard Keown, as he directed the Australian premiere production of John Harrison's *Holidays* at Peridot Theatre in Melbourne. Later, Susan had the privilege of directing the Australian premiere production of Timothy Daly's *Beach: A Theatrical Fantasia* with a young cast.

Always passionate about the arts and wanting to share her knowledge with young people, Susan completed a postgraduate Bachelor of Education: Primary and Secondary, at Deakin University and was privileged to learn from the expertise of her amazing lecturers: Dr Jo O'Mara and Dr Jo Raphael.

Susan has taught professionally in primary and secondary schools for more than a decade and has undertaken the role of Head of Drama. She has also written a number of drama and literacy articles for academic publications and mentored pre-service and practising teachers. Susan has presented at state and national conferences in drama and literacy education, including at the Victorian College of the Arts, the University of Melbourne and at the Queensland University of Technology in Brisbane and has also worked as an executive committee member for Drama Victoria.

As time progressed, Susan immersed herself in the adventures of play writing with the intention of developing works for young adults to explore in the classroom or youth theatre settings. This led to the development of her play: *Broken World*, which was published by RMDesigned in 2013. The play was launched at the joint AATE/ALEA National Conference and positively reviewed by the Children's Book Council of Australia. RMDesigned also published Susan's second play, *Indigo's Haven* in 2016.

Susan has also written a range of publications, which have been published at Vocal Media in the U.S.A. These include, Susan's poems: *Grandpa Ben's Mysterious Notebook: A Tale*; *A Day Spent: the Playful Thoughts of a Tired Mind*; *My Nature Spirit: A Poem Celebrating my Connection with Nature*; *Is Summer Still Aglow Within Thy Heart?: The Eternal Shore of Summer Love*; *Winter's Breath: Mother Nature's Precious Time* and *Heart's Land*, along with her short stories: *Paper Jilu: A Journey of Her Notes*; *Gail's Red Horizon: A Fantastical Adventure*; *Hidden Magic: Part 1*; *Peonies for Masha: Her Journey Home* (shortlisted as a finalist in the Vocal+ Fiction Awards, 2022); *Stay* and *Tace's Lost Spirit: Searching for Vie*.

Susan is an honoured recipient of the prestigious *Award for Special Civic Service*, which was presented to her by the Mayor of Richmond, Victoria, for her extensive civic contributions to the city of Richmond and the Richmond City Council. The Award particularly recognises her outstanding efforts in assisting young people through her work on the Richmond Youth Work Project and the Richmond Youth Council.

In 2020, Susan founded Story Playscapes, her writing and publishing business. It was here that she became globally renown for delving into her playscapes when developing her writing. Susan's written works are highly respected by a dedicated global audience.

As an author, theatre practitioner and educator, Susan brings a wealth of knowledge to Story Playscapes. She is passionate about empowering literacy development in her global readership. Susan is also big hearted in her discussions on social media, where she fosters a love for reading and discovery in her readers.

In 2022, Susan was privileged to collaborate with the world class designer, Ryan Marshall, on the book design of her debut novel: *Makeshift Girl: The Secret Heritage Trail*, which was initially published in 2023 and released across the globe.

In 2023, Susan continued her collaboration with Ryan Marshall and was honoured that he designed her play publications for young adults: *Fleur of Yesterday* and *All the Hope We Carry*. As the first two plays released in Susan's new Theatre Playscapes series, they officially present her monumental achievement: her new Theatre Playscapes theatrical style, developed for young performers, to readers and theatre makers around the world.

In 2024, Susan is excited to share her novel: *Adira and the Dark Horse*, designed by Ryan Marshall and published by Story Playscapes. It is the first book for adults in the new Adira Cazon Literary Mystery series. An atmospheric and gripping page turner, it unravels private detective Adira Cazon's journey as she attempts to outwit the dangerous dark horse. In Susan's exclusive collection of 30 poems for adults: *Bare Spirit: The Selected Poems of Susan Marshall*, (also designed by Ryan Marshall and published by Story Playscapes), she further reveals how her attunement to the energetic motions of her lifeworlds, enables her to set the spirit alight. Susan's sensual verse draws upon breathtaking imagery to distil and transcend single moments, which can arise the 'bare spirit' from within.

Acknowledgements

It is a privilege to be able to wander across our diverse, beautiful world and to continue to grow spiritually. I am thankful to each and every person I have met along my life journey so far. To be touched with the joy of another's way of life and to connect with them is truly rewarding. Through deepened knowledge of the world and via my own spiritual connections with its energetic motions (my playscapes), I have grown spiritually at an exponential scale.

A very special thank you to Ryan Marshall for being so continually attuned to my spiritual presence and my writing. It is such a wonderful experience to be able to share my visions and passions with someone as talented as Ryan. He is an amazing, world class designer and a wonderful husband. His professional design work on this book is exceptional and speaks to me deeply. Thank you.

It has been a spiritually awakening journey, sharing my poetry with our readers via our My Story Meadow project. Through sharing, I have deepened my understandings of how to communicate with others through writing. I am committed to continuing to provide global literacy development opportunities to our readers. It is touching to have such interest and support by each and every reader who has connected with me. I will always be eternally grateful for your kindness and support in my life journey. Thank you.

About the Book Designer

Ryan Marshall is a professional graphic designer, photographer and illustrator, with more than 20 years of experience in designing a broad range of monographs, trade and fiction publications for world-leading professionals in the arts, design, photographic, automotive, landscape design and architectural industries.

Ryan has applied his unique technical skill set to the design and creation of hundreds of titles and includes significant contributions to international bestselling publications and series.

Ryan has collaborated with Susan Marshall and designed Story Playscapes' publications: *Makeshift Girl: The Secret Heritage Trail, Fleur of Yesterday* and *All the Hope We Carry*.

In 2024, Ryan has collaborated with Susan Marshall and Story Playscapes on the publication: *Adira and the Dark Horse* by Susan Marshall. He is honoured to bring his highly proficient design and technical expertise to the book design of Susan's exclusive poetry collection for adults: *Bare Spirit: The Selected Poems of Susan Marshall*.

It is a rewarding experience for Ryan to collaborate with Susan and to bring her wonderful stories to the printed page for readers to discover and enjoy!

About Story Playscapes

Story Playscapes, established in 2020, is an Australian writing and publishing business founded by Australian Author, Susan Marshall.

The business is dedicated to promoting positive approaches to literacy development. It nurtures a global readership by actively sharing Susan Marshall's diverse range of written works on its website and via print and ebook publications.

In 2023, Story Playscapes released its premiere publication: *Makeshift Girl: The Secret Heritage Trail* by Susan Marshall. In the same year, Story Playscapes also released *Fleur of Yesterday and All the Hope We Carry,* the first two plays written by Susan Marshall in her exciting, monumental Theatre Playscapes series for young adults around the globe.

In 2024, Story Playscapes was privileged to produce the publication: *Adira and the Dark Horse* by Susan Marshall. It is the first book for adults in the new Adira Cazon Literary Mystery series. An atmospheric and gripping page turner, it unravels private detective Adira Cazon's journey as she attempts to outwit the dangerous dark horse.

Story Playscapes is honoured to release *Bare Spirit: The Selected Poems of Susan Marshall,* an exclusive collection of 30 poems for adults, which further reveals how her attunement to the energetic motions of her lifeworlds, enables her to set the spirit alight. Susan's sensual verse draws upon breathtaking imagery to distil and transcend single moments, which can arise the 'bare spirit' from within.

DISCOVER THE STORY

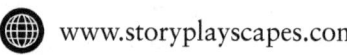 www.storyplayscapes.com

Facebook: /storyplayscapes

Instagram: @storyplayscapes

Also by Susan Marshall:

Will Adira outwit the dark horse?

Adira Cazon grew up with her parents in Mira, an unsympathetic empire, fuelled by the wealth of its silk trade. In a world of long held resistance against empirical power, Adira discovered that she was a desired asset for the dangerous dark horse. After witnessing her own family tragedy, Adira was assisted by her mother to seek safe refuge.

Now 23, Adira is a trained private detective, who has built her life in Redbank. As the presence of the dark horse pervades the industrial city's society, Adira swears to protect Girl, a silk merchant from Mira, who is hiding in Redbank. News soon arrives that Adira's mother has been declared a missing person and that significant heritage silk apparel have been stolen from Mira. As she investigates an evolving illegal trade operation, Adira is determined to outwit the dark horse who is hunting her down.

Interweaving the narrative of Adira's journey with the secrets kept by other courageous women who also confronted the dangerous powers dominating the silk trade routes of past and present, *Adira and the Dark Horse* by award-winning Susan Marshall, is an atmospheric and gripping page turner in search of the truth.

Title: Adira and the Dark Horse   **Series:** An Adira Cazon Literary Mystery
ISBN: 9780645404159

NOW AVAILABLE AT ALL GOOD BOOKSTORES AROUND THE GLOBE.